PIANO · VOCAL · GUITAR **2ND EDITION**

Love Songs of the '30s

Contents

ISBN 0-7935-4441-6

HAL•LEONARD
CORPORATION

7777 W. BLUEMOUND RD. P.O. BOX 13819 MILWAUKEE, WI 53213

Visit Hal Leonard Online at
www.halleonard.com

ALL THE THINGS YOU ARE

from VERY WARM FOR MAY

Lyrics by OSCAR HAMMERSTEIN II
Music by JEROME KERN

Time and a - gain I've longed for ad - ven - ture, some - thing to make my

heart beat the fast - er. What did I long for? I nev - er real - ly

knew.   Find - ing your love, I've found my ad - ven - ture;

BODY AND SOUL

Words by EDWARD HEYMAN,
ROBERT SOUR and FRANK EYTON
Music by JOHN GREEN

Expressively

CHANGE PARTNERS

from the RKO Radio Motion Picture CAREFREE

Words and Music by
IRVING BERLIN

danced with him since the mu - sic be - gan.

Won't you change part - ners and

dance with me? Must you dance

quite so close

Ask him to sit this one out, and while you're a - lone

I'll tell the wait - er to tell him he's

want - ed on the tel - e - phone. You've been locked

in his arms

CHEEK TO CHEEK

from the RKO Radio Motion Picture TOP HAT

Words and Music by
IRVING BERLIN

DREAM A LITTLE DREAM OF ME

Words by GUS KAHN
Music by WILBUR SCHWANDT and FABIAN ANDREE

DON'T BLAME ME

Words by DOROTHY FIELDS
Music by JIMMY McHUGH

A FINE ROMANCE

from SWING TIME

Words by DOROTHY FIELDS
Music by JEROME KERN

THE FOLKS WHO LIVE ON THE HILL

from HIGH, WIDE AND HANDSOME

Lyrics by OSCAR HAMMERSTEIN II
Music by JEROME KERN

HOW DEEP IS THE OCEAN
(How High Is the Sky)

Words and Music by
IRVING BERLIN

41

THE GLORY OF LOVE
from GUESS WHO'S COMING TO DINNER

Words and Music by
BILLY HILL

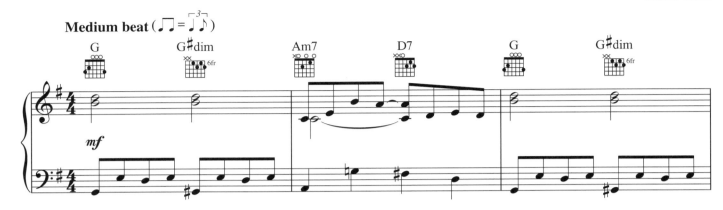

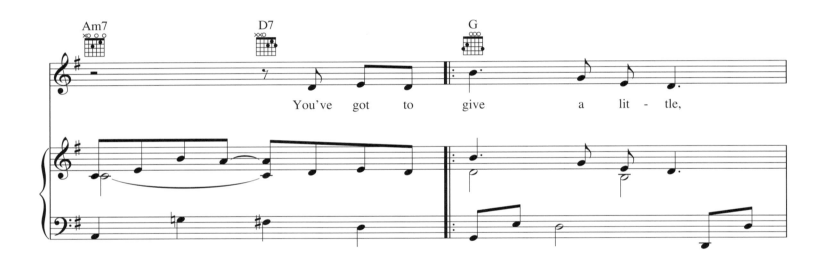

You've got to give a lit-tle,

take a lit-tle, and let your poor heart break a lit-tle.

HEART AND SOUL

from the Paramount Short Subject A SONG IS BORN

Words by FRANK LOESSER
Music by HOAGY CARMICHAEL

Moderately, lightly rhythmical

I DON'T KNOW WHY
(I Just Do)

Lyric by ROY TURK
Music by FRED E. AHLERT

I'LL BE SEEING YOU

from RIGHT THIS WAY

Lyric by IRVING KAHAL
Music by SAMMY FAIN

Moderately

Ca-the-dral bells were toll - ing _____ and our hearts sang on, _____ was it the spell of Par - is _____ or the A - pril dawn? _____ Who knows, _____ if we shall meet a - gain? _____

I'VE GOT MY LOVE TO KEEP ME WARM

from the 20th Century Fox Motion Picture ON THE AVENUE

Words and Music by
IRVING BERLIN

Bright jump tempo

I'VE GOT THE WORLD ON A STRING

Lyric by TED KOEHLER
Music by HAROLD ARLEN

Mer - ry month of May, sun - ny

I'VE GOT YOU UNDER MY SKIN

from BORN TO DANCE

Words and Music by
COLE PORTER

66

But each time I do, just the thought of you makes me stop be-fore I be-gin, 'cause I've got you un-der my skin. I've

IN A SENTIMENTAL MOOD

Words and Music by DUKE ELLINGTON,
IRVING MILLS and MANNY KURTZ

ISN'T IT ROMANTIC?
from the Paramount Picture LOVE ME TONIGHT

Words by LORENZ HART
Music by RICHARD RODGERS

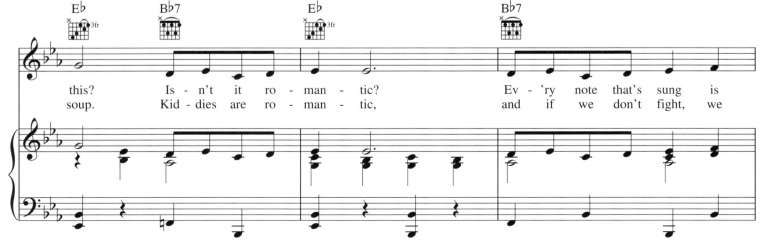

IN THE STILL OF THE NIGHT

from ROSALIE
from NIGHT AND DAY

Words and Music by
COLE PORTER

night?

JUNE IN JANUARY

from the Paramount Picture HERE IS MY HEART

Words and Music by LEO ROBIN
and RALPH RAINGER

LOVER
from the Paramount Picture LOVE ME TONIGHT

Words by LORENZ HART
Music by RICHARD RODGERS

When you held your hand to my heart, dear, you did some - thing grand to my heart, and we played the scene to per - fec - tion, _____ though we did - n't have time to re - hearse. _____

THE LADY'S IN LOVE WITH YOU

from the Paramount Picture SOME LIKE IT HOT

Words by FRANK LOESSER
Music by BURTON LANE

LET'S FALL IN LOVE

Words by TED KOEHLER
Music by HAROLD ARLEN

LOVE IS JUST AROUND THE CORNER

from the Paramount Picture HERE IS MY HEART

Words and Music by LEO ROBIN
and LEWIS E. GENSLER

Brightly, not too fast

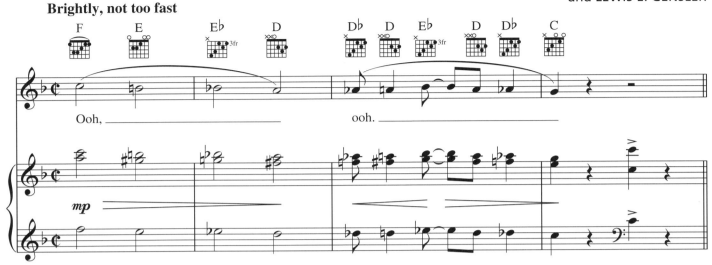

Ooh, _____ ooh. _____

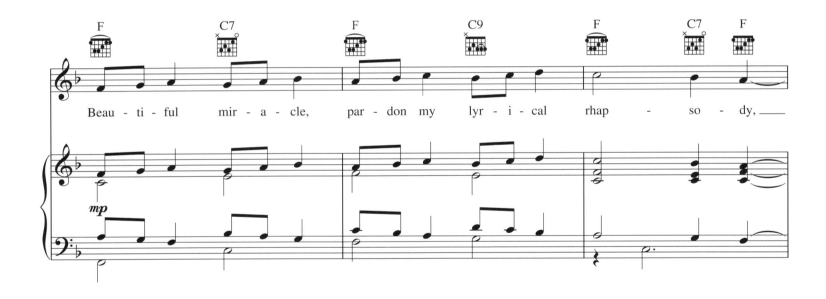

Beau - ti - ful mir - a - cle, par - don my lyr - i - cal rhap - so - dy, ___

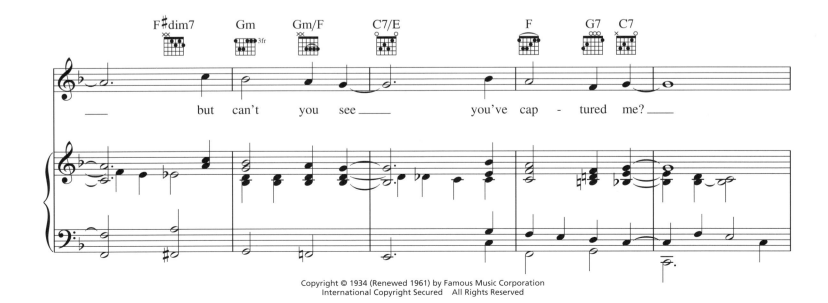

___ but can't you see ___ you've cap - tured me? ___

LOVELY TO LOOK AT

from ROBERTA

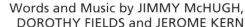

Words and Music by JIMMY McHUGH,
DOROTHY FIELDS and JEROME KERN

106

thrill - ing to hold you ter - ri - bly tight.___

For we're to - geth - er, the moon is new, and

oh, it's love - ly to look at you to - night!___

You're

MEMORIES OF YOU
from THE BENNY GOODMAN STORY

Lyric by ANDY RAZAF
Music by EUBIE BLAKE

MOONGLOW

Words and Music by WILL HUDSON,
EDDIE DE LANGE and IRVING MILLS

MY BABY JUST CARES FOR ME

from WHOOPEE!

Lyrics by GUS KAHN
Music by WALTER DONALDSON

some one loves_ me too. _____ Gues it's hard for

you to see_ just what an - y - one_ can see in me,_ but it

sim - ply goes to prove what love_ can do. _____

My ba - by don't care for shows, my ba - by don't
My ba - by's no Gil - bert fan, Ron Col - man is

MY FUNNY VALENTINE

from BABES IN ARMS

Words by LORENZ HART
Music by RICHARD RODGERS

8vb

MY IDEAL
from the Paramount Picture PLAYBOY OF PARIS

Words by LEO ROBIN
Music by RICHARD A. WHITING and NEWELL CHASE

MY ROMANCE

from JUMBO

Words by LORENZ HART
Music by RICHARD RODGERS

SEPTEMBER SONG

from the Musical Play KNICKERBOCKER HOLIDAY

Words by MAXWELL ANDERSON
Music by KURT WEILL

THE SONG IS YOU
from MUSIC IN THE AIR

Lyrics by OSCAR HAMMERSTEIN II
Music by JEROME KERN

STARDUST

Words by MITCHELL PARISH
Music by HOAGY CARMICHAEL

THERE'S A SMALL HOTEL
from ON YOUR TOES

Words by LORENZ HART
Music by RICHARD RODGERS

THERE IS NO GREATER LOVE

Words by MARTY SYMES
Music by ISHAM JONES

THESE FOOLISH THINGS
(Remind Me of You)

Words by HOLT MARVELL
Music by JACK STRACHEY

153

THIS CAN'T BE LOVE

from THE BOYS FROM SYRACUSE

Words by LORENZ HART
Music by RICHARD RODGERS

THE TOUCH OF YOUR HAND

from ROBERTA

Words by OTTO HARBACH
Music by JEROME KERN

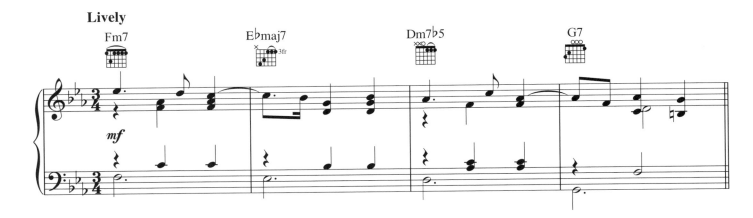

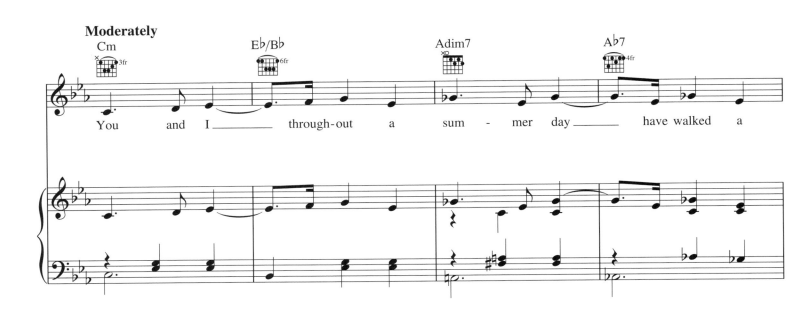

You and I _____ through-out a sum - mer day _____ have walked a

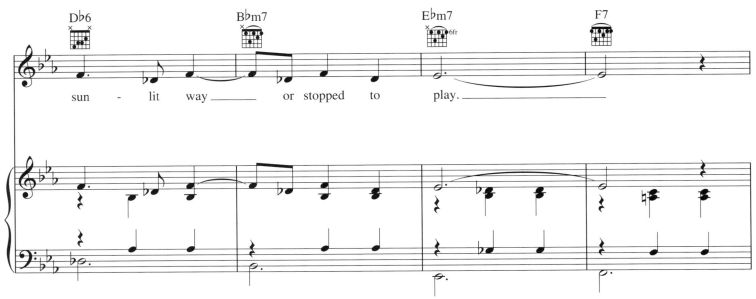

sun - lit way _____ or stopped to play. _____

THE VERY THOUGHT OF YOU

Words and Music by
RAY NOBLE

I don't need your pho-to-graph, _____
I hold you re-spon-si-ble, _____

_____ to keep _____ by my bed;
_____ I'll take _____ it to law,

Your pic-ture is
I nev-er have

al-ways in _____ my head. _____
felt like this _____ be-fore. _____

THE WAY YOU LOOK TONIGHT

from SWING TIME

Words by DOROTHY FIELDS
Music by JEROME KERN

YOU ARE TOO BEAUTIFUL
from HALLELUJAH, I'M A BUM

Words by LORENZ HART
Music by RICHARD RODGERS

WHAT A DIFF'RENCE A DAY MADE

English Words by STANLEY ADAMS
Music and Spanish Words by MARIA GREVER